NO SWEET
WITHOUT
BRINE

Poems

CYNTHIA
MANICK

AMISTAD
An Imprint of HarperCollins*Publishers*

The credits on pages 129–30 constitute a continuation of this copyright page.

NO SWEET WITHOUT BRINE. Copyright © 2023 by Cynthia Manick. All rights reserved. Printed in the United States of America. No part of this book may be used or reproduced in any manner whatsoever without written permission except in the case of brief quotations embodied in critical articles and reviews. For information, address HarperCollins Publishers, 195 Broadway, New York, NY 10007.

HarperCollins books may be purchased for educational, business, or sales promotional use. For information, please email the Special Markets Department at SPsales@harpercollins.com.

FIRST EDITION

Designed by THE COSMIC LION

Library of Congress Cataloging-in-Publication Data is available upon request.

ISBN 978-0-06-324430-6

23 24 25 26 27 LBC 5 4 3 2 1

NO SWEET WITHOUT BRINE

Also by Cynthia Manick

The Future of Black: Afrofuturism,
Black Comics & Superhero Poetry

Soul Sister Revue:
A Poetry Compilation

Blue Hallelujahs

Contents

Sin Is a Good Hymn

If We Should, Who Will Fly After Us

Tanka for a Beginning

I keep forgetting
how many people love me—
these wild hands plucked from
wild waters, Dixie roads, two
Afro clouds bursting one night

SELF-PORTRAITS
AND
OTHER SKIES

Always Use a Gold Crayon
to Color Yourself In

We little brown peas   we awkward canaries
       black apostrophes that god made
          know how to love ourselves small

I remember the hunch of middle school shoulders
       chasing beauty like it was the moon or
          the last buffalo

There were caramel boys in red Jordans
       mouths full of recess and celebrity names—
          Lisa Bonet   Vanity   Rae Dawn Chong

There must've been secrets in the forming
       ingredients offered only to a select few
          or perhaps a crossroads deal of ash
          and lullabies

Hair—not a mining town of frizz—check
       skin—shades of toasted coconut—check
          body—size 6 glitter bomb that never
          sweats—check

We dark wonders   we blooming nightshades
       passed the hot comb sizzle and splatter
          to permed crack tresses and neutralizers

Dear Madame C   Dear Satin Bonnet
protect us from natural   rain and cotton
plant yourself so deep   we crave you
always

Our hands are question marks   this need doesn't wane
like starlight or an Achilles ache that's never done
I blame   a lot of people

For listing all the ways we   are a problem
for the abundance of beige crayons
the heavy smirks towards gap-
toothed smiles

I am forging a bonfire surrounded by soil and vowels
Grace Jones   fish fries   cocoa butter
brown and black streaks missing from the
rainbow

We so fly   no voodoo required
we so fly   call us constellation
we so fly   the sun be jealous

Self-Portrait No. 1
(On Becoming Light)

I've tried to learn
what makes the blood run,
churn the molecules
until a hurricane stirs my name,
why I often want to rage—
leap atop windowsills
with the stride
of an Amazonian or Zulu princess
or feel energy
pounding in my hands.

My sisters' most terrifying
memory is of Granddaddy—
her in a daisy spring dress
flying high on the swings,
pink jelly sandals in the sky.
Him and the gasp
of a long-ass rifle, the black
rat snake in its last rattle.

She remembers my grandma's
smile on her forehead,
pickles and its juice in a jar

mopped tears, butter cookies
and fresh teat milk.

People say she has my grandma's
smile; and I Granddaddy's
trigger finger.

Ode to *JET* Magazine (When You Be a Rainbow with a Streak of Black)

Momma lived between two large
stones; Daddy with his dip-lean
walk and three mouths hungry. But on
special nights she'd draw a bath
of Epsom salt, Avon (blue), turn to *JET*
magazine to see a door in every word.

> *Dear Prince,*
> *I miss your Afro cause*
> *real funk needs room*
> *to breathe, space to map*
> *joints, sprout octaves*
> *like a volcano.*

Daddy called it mailbox ambush; Redd
Foxx the Negro bible. *JET* arrived
and Mama was more bite than talk. Quick
eats meant franks with Campbell's
pork'n'beans or spaghetti with just sauce.
We knew to quiet our hides with TV
reruns and peeled tangerines.

> *Dear Beauty of the Week,*
> *when Mama's not*
> *lookin, Daddy calls you*

speckled sin
with a side of gravy.

This is how we learn—
curve, spin, and dip our weave
blue eye shadow the classy way
worry about Jesse Jackson's mom
did you hear about Marvin Gaye's dad
roll that back-of-the-bus fury into want . . .
of pink Cadillacs, toned ridges
of Angela Bassett's arms.

> *Dear Don Cornelius,*
> *Where do you buy your*
> *glasses? Do they have*
> *X-ray vision? Can you see*
> *steps of the Congo*
> *in the* Soul Train *line?*

I bring Momma the news with a cup
of tea, explain that *JET* is done with
5 x 7 shapes, the perfect fit for bags, make-
shift church fans, and flyswatters.
She looks years behind—
to Emmett Till's face pressed in pages,
look what they did to that baby . . .
to Rosa's purse clutched in hand,
tucks a printed page by her breast for keeping.

Dear JET *Weddings*
I like the couples you
choose. Do they eat
from the same Luther
Vandross love tree? All
their teeth sparkle
in the dark.

I Try to Imagine Them Smitten

I've never seen my parents' kiss
or try to be the silver
dollar in each other's pocket.

In one photo they're on
a green loveseat—the plastic
cover looks sweaty to touch.
Dad is standing to the side,
Afro Sheen bright as paint,
mouth curved to sing *something*
alive. My mom is seated,
brown legs crossed and bare.

Clasping hands they hold close
those disappearing things—
slow dancing to Marvin's
mercy mercy me
a mumbling river
a blue patchwork quilt its
ends ragged to touch
and a bowl of honeydew melon
saved for midnight when
the kids are asleep.

Did they ever touch
like bathwater on ankles

or whisper thoughts so hot
only the dust could hear?

I try to imagine them smitten
past the slammed doors
past the obsidian quiet
to side glances and half-tones,
but maybe it only happened once
in a South Carolina grove
where only the moon could see.

MTA Transit Exam Attempt #4

• •

One night I hear my father's
voice shaking out
if u   want   a   peal our
eval u   ation   of
ur m   ploy   ment   hist   ory
like his tongue are magpies
needing to be trained.

When I step in the kitchen
he becomes a silent movie,
but there are no Black fathers
in silent movies.

Later I discover he takes
the exam a fifth, sixth,
and eighth time
un   der   soup   er   vision
pre   pair   track   and   road
until muzzled he stopped—

thrashing on the hook
trying to swim upstream
to pay with a-little-
somethin-left-over.

And I learn to hide
my shimmer
forget spelling bees
star-sticker reading charts,
and test score smiles
thinking them Master tools
to be used only in secret.

Tanka Suite on Survival

1

I see yellow peeps
Preachers pulpit, Mary Jane
shoes and Burn-ingham.
Four little ghost girls smiling
singing, covered in light soot.

2

Remind me not to
linger on whiskeyed words dropped
past midnight—they hem
a body in like yucca
trees; scar easily as love.

3

Lately I've tried not
to record the names of our
dead. Since Katrina
they sprout out walls and cover
floors like pink insulation.

4

I offer you dark
crooks of my elbow, well-washed
copper shells. Don't drink
too deep, you'll unearth seven
layers of grit, soul, and blade.

Litany for My Fears and Questions

after Audre Lorde

· ·

For those of us getting used to writing poems—

— for the dead for the dead
— for rainbows without a streak of black
— for gerbera daisies that wilt quickly
— for silence so quiet you tilt like earth's axis
  like that day in September when the phones
  rang and rang
  and you learned that charred wood is stronger
  than most barks
— Does love taste like sweetgrass?
— Can I be mad as love as sweetgrass?
— Does this jump in the blood mean I'm having a heart
  attack . . . a heartbreak . . or a heart's fury between
  dawns?
— Can a mouth be starved for the sun?
— How many fibroids is too many?
— Can I take 3 Aleves instead of 2?

For those of us expected to beautify—

— what's hemmed in
— the latest numbers in our zip codes
— questions on God . . . particles . . . boredom . . .
— conversations with the town crier . . . I mean our
  mothers glued to the phone to relay names of the
  sick, they fall like em dashes or brittle teeth

— When will scientists name this new emotion?
— Is it wrong to want a storm named after you?
— Can a 3 am phone call be good news—
    news so jubilant that our lungs expound 6 liters of
    air?

  Let this be the last time we mourn

— or dream of beasts
— or a beach full of a 100 brown turtles
    retracted in their shells.

Is This Your Sky or Mine?

• •

I try to quantify what we inherit—
dancers' legs that know how to roam
but be church pious by morning,
the ability to fold shirts into a perfect square,
or the street walk that says *I'm a willing
dove but need no man or pierced jewelry.*

I've learned that when the grease bubbles,
you put the fish in, nail polish will
stop a run in any stocking. Did you
mean to build something that lasts?

I want to give you a cinematic back-
story, far from southern charms and swamp
boys, but I can't picture your shift
from girl to woman, mine but not, strong
but not. You tuck the girdle in so
the belly doesn't roll, curl the feet like
commas. The body just births more
questions and that's my future.

I've always been quietly wild and I'm
sorry for talking too fast, too much, but
I'm trying to catch all the unanchored parts
of you—rough magic, farm tales of

double-yolked eggs, a collage of memories
trapped in photo albums because you
rarely cover old ground. I think every
poem I write is about you, Mama.

Eintou for Possibility

I think
the gap between
my teeth is actually
a portal. A world where all the
gaps meet—gossip about
peas, whistling,
and stars.

I Learned to Be a Lady

On summer mornings I craved
blackened foot heels
and backyard lakes, water-
shrinking barrettes
to an almost-paradise
crown of four little knots
on my head. And layers
of dirt from days
of playing so hard I
sprawled, a dizzy
starfish with five points
ready to slay—mongrel
trees, trap dragon hide,
or moonwalk with cherry-
lime blow-pop in hand.
But one day
an older aunt says—
girl, you better clean
those dirty feet so the
devil don't know
your name. Putting a lid
on thirst, I copy grace
from church ladies, TV mom
Phylicia Rashad, and Kim
Fields as Tootie. Turn

to bottles to smooth hair-
line edge, stockings
baptized, and scabbed lady legs.
Be glossy-lipped, use Dark
& Lovely, unfurl feet in the earth
only in the shade where
no one else can see.

Urban Tumbleweed

• •

At first, I thought it was just apertures
and light, my father lifting the trunk—
shades of my suitcases and his back

bent down. Our ritual of airport
pickups and half-speak normal—
except for a well-used baby stroller

covered like an almost secret.
He wades away from my gaze,
questions the weight of brass arrows.

Am I urban tumbleweed?
Remembered only through side
glances, green M&M's fingerprints

I smudged on his dashboard as a child.
Is he making new tribes? Swiping
teeth from pillows, leaving dollar

bills instead of quarters. I know
he stopped smoking recently but
in pictures my five-year-old barrettes

smell like Newports, fast food, Al
Green's "Love and Happiness," a
loud silence at the kitchen table.

Has he taken them to kindergarten
with pencil cases shaped like trains?
Do they have nicknames? My mouth

tries to open, capture the ghost family
that hovers—but instead we talk of planes
touching down so we don't have to speak.

Pretending Is Like Breathing

· ·

At the supermarket family stories fall
out like burnt green pennies. With a Bible-
sized coupon holder my aunt
knows the manager specials,
the days half-price roast is coming,
and her favorite cashier's vacation
schedule. Relays these while checking off
her list of "must haves" and telling
me of her own mother's quest for under-
priced soup. I try to follow the tale,
nodding like a brown Cabbage Patch
doll that doesn't blink, asking follow-up
questions, but I keep glancing at her list.
The cursive identical to the *i just want*
in a diary I found in a box of forgotten
things—as if moths had unraveled some
hems and created nets across pages. It said,
he's with her again . . . sniffing her
coon shine . . . i just want what's mine
. . . what he promised . . . i just want
my heart . . . the kids . . . we'll have
no money. I remember closing the fire—
wanting to find a wall or wooded
place to hide the book, a place little
brothers and cousins don't go. But now

she's telling me stories of other supermarkets.
Their flimsy bags too thin for a 2-liter
bottle of Coke and Gain detergent; her steady
fear of things spilling out.

How You Livin?

• •

like the air ain't filled with
coarse wind chimes
sirens loud as a jet in flight

the quick jabs
of a couple arguing about cheese
and face masks
and children at borders
borders of language
and knotted bellies

I tell you
it's hard to sleep
when the news is a bare-
skinned sidekick

I try to harden my shell
make it marble
filled with filament
and nails

but how you livin
among the salt, ash, and slate
at your doorstep—all this
grit under your eyelids

3 am and the Moon is Curled like a "C"

* *

And I didn't dream of coffins today
or the scattering of names or trees
I can never recall. Instead there was a silver
dog chasing joy in the shape of a hat,
a long-dead cousin eating Jack and Jill
cookies, and my hands held fistfuls
of not-yet-ripe tomatoes that needed a dark
place or bag to become true.
Do I need to go shopping or check on a relative?
The dream book says tomatoes symbolize harmony
but my mind wonders how long it takes
for a star to burn out
and if its last beats are like a bare-
foot heart in love for the first time.
I once read that Black poets write love poems the least,
as if we're too busy swallowing
mouthfuls of dusks
tallying wounds, knowing how often
atoms fissure and our bodies part.
But can we not do both?
Banish the lines—go braless and numb,
fumble in the dark with a sweat so sweet
he or she is well-fed.
Fill pages with bathwater and breaths ungraceful.
Movement like a train
of yellow flowers because it's what we saw

on our very first date. In another dream,
I see a fleet of newly painted dove-
white subway trains—ugly beautiful,
as if a ghost threw pure light.
People both alive and passed are full
of bright colors I can't name.
They move so smooth my ear
barely recognizes the revolving jubilee,
the sky inside all of their hands.

I Wish the Trees Could Sway to Marvin and Aretha

• •

because sometimes I forget / soil / can do more than hold/
wooden or metal boxes / it pulls on elements / my shins have
long forgotten / there are seven / different words for dirt / in
French / we hear / what is left / in the woods / children with
twelve / fingers or webbed toes / I used to pray / for normal
appendages / I often stopped / myself from talking out loud /
singing where others / could hear / but we know / of *hushed*
tales / *somebody's callin* / *my name* / about where wounds /
used to go / to the trees / swinging / someone's Black uncle /
or son / sometime daughter's under / steady stars / bright
as birth / day candles / we can't blow / but let's not talk / of
dark / histories / of how you and I / are still alive / like three-
flowered maples or perennials / unculled / or how standing /
on a hilltop / just over there / with headphones / a seashell of
Motown / and Aretha / you forget the universe / is expanding /
as if the gods are / tired of our sand / and stone / bones / brutal
ozone's / the oldest tree / is over 4,000 years old / but what if /
the bark doesn't hold / like it used to / the bloom turns shallow /
cause you can die / from survival you know / it's like working
three jobs / the weight of limbs / in winter / so that tree / has
breathed a lot / of shit / geographic shadows / but soul music /
can be / a prayer / and what if / it could reach / every spore /
every carbonated leaf / note / pollinating dreams like bees /
down to the root / until every bark / vibrates / under our
palms / and what if Marvin / and Aretha / can make them
remember / what love sounds like / and all the wild things /
come so close / the trees no longer die / standing up

Self-Portrait No. 5
(Phoenix and Lullabies)

Some people think I was born
savage   biting at hands clouds and daggers
with no softness to be found   but I contain
whispers   bright coral beads stacked
the language of blood jostling against itself,
coconut oil   curves molded by my mother's thumb
broad bones and something wild.   Sometimes I'm
a brown belly   songbird   who knows the tongue
can be a land not beaten   the hot arch ache
in someone's back   while the TV's on,
or it can be a pistol.   It covers all   my gristle barbs
blue and yellow howls   and the rag doll heart,
where I shook off my father's   baritone
the day he left.   I turn brine lake   that never stirs
the same way twice   salty assholes and smiles
boiled over.   It's not a lie to say   that I'm still learning
to love   the frames of undressed trees   my glasses
the Medusa hair that defies   every comb   red
pomegranates   my baby self   the little girl inside
who still craves   model trains   *Josie and the
Pussycats* cartoon   and wonders about the spaces
between the teeth and the ribs.

I Want Us Living,
Not Just Alive

Rx for Little Black Girls

Main Ingredient: collective memory. the other side of every copper coin. a mother's grief rolls into a ball until the edges meet. think of translucent fried onion in its own juices. some place it in a glass jar. others throw it like bathwater.

Common Uses Include:
falling into beauty. all is awe and tender. but Jemima was a daughter once too. shake the hands from your skirts. take this Rx before walking alone in the woods or cement jungle in a dress people claim is too tight, too loose, too you.

Before Using: know you come from a long line of women. some covet the shine of your darkness; others shear their hair from the root cause they can't handle the skin. cities and cosmetics are made of this.

Directives: imagine a reed flute. the tune will come when called. place it in the bottom of every Solo cup. Store it in your braids, deep enough to pass a TSA airport inspection.

Be Advised: you will no longer speak quietly at coffins. great dancers learn to speak without a mouth. be sister, little miss, ms., momma, or wife when you choose. but move with all the air your body can hold.

Warning: if overdose suspected, shake the memory from your hair. know how to leave, love, skip without thought. eat a hot dog or banana like nobody's watching. if taken by a culture appropriator, a side-eye will commence. stones gather in wombs to those who want all our sway but none of the pain.

Possible Side Effects: you become a public danger because you can sing anything alive. make sense without light. carve your name anywhere through pen, voice, or axe.

Livin Flush

for Mama Lucille

• •

On payday we sweet
everything like our number
done hit—our knees be spry,
but tomorrow we'll eat dry
tuna like it's caviar.

Girls Like Me Are Made Of . . .

Bread crumbs, flour filling,
        ginger for eyes and a splash

of rum and gasoline. Full bodied
        I'll toddle off to school, stuffing

my stomach with Berenstain Bears,
        Little Miss Stubborn or Bossy.

An older sibling watches but
        doesn't hold my hand cause grit

starts early, like knowing names
        of tincture plants and the sweetness

of red candy. When I crave copper tins,
        tea and curse words,

douse me with white owl feathers
        so I'll know what a soul tastes like.

Then plait my hair in matching barrettes
        the size of blue and gold fireflies.

At night I'll feel them moving,
        and learn the need of dreams.

Baby, What's Your Favorite Body Part?

••

a blue   collar man asks
with his mouth   shaped like
a preacher's   gaze the size
of wishes.   and part of my rib
cuts open   something heavier
than a sequoia   tree settles
in its place. gone   is the practiced
Josephine Baker   head tilt   my
imagined swagger   of a bolero
singer   or flamenco star.   I hear
damnn, like a buttered   biscuit,
I wish she'd grease my . . . who knows
how not   to blossom?   be well-
aimed lightning to a sweaty
wrist   kick like a dark   flank
the family   friend   who hugs you
just   a little too tight.   those who say
mine when you   are silent.   I want
these dancer's legs   pulled from
a womb to know when   to speak,
run   be cocoa-butter   shine
and woman.   I wish those men
a hex they can't   breath out
adrenaline like arsenic   loose stool

a wraith of mothers   named Caroline
and Mary   a pot of sisters   called
Princess and Mya   following them home
whenever   it's dark

Dear Future Body
(Keep Your Skin Thickk)

. .

Yesterday my legs were propped
in stirrups as the gyno said,
You should go on The Biggest Loser.
I heard cities at the skull base
stuttering over each other,
vine and vowels of *your rolls*
and the *garden under your chin.*
The implied real estate of—
don't you want to be beautiful?
We have known the trap
of nameless and hungry
BMI indexes.
Dear God and sample-size fashion,
I escape and get caught
in the same geography again and again,
unmade and remade.
I forget I am more than a house
of great bones,
of Vaseline and Werther's Originals.
The Caucasity of a well-meaning
she has such a pretty face.
I'm writing to tell you about
a type of war,
people carving the cavalry horses
to survive

the outline of social media
models and how many calories
is this bottle of air?
What else can we eliminate?
I always thought the planet Pluto
was a Black girl,
now downgraded and mostly out.
Dear Future Body,
take a break today.
Tell me—how are your kisses?
Sometimes they give birth
to promises,
a season in the word,
oil and oxygen at the ready.
Are you someone's night bloom?
Remember to trace what remains,
the prayers your mouth learns.
I want us living, not just alive.

A Particular Truth About Grown Folks' Grits

for Rachel and Tyehimba

I have eaten grits in the summer.
Boiled the water first, prepping for a type
of colorless baby, not too far from sun-
flower seeds and peanut shells.

What it must feel like to be salt,
a wooden spoon knowing there is beauty
in the life of flowers—no I mean
natural things with a "best used by" or
expiration date, as if we're born waiting
to go back to ground—no I mean Disney talks
about the circle-of-life but no character
has both parents alive enough to pay rent.

I have added grits to barely black pots
in fall, after hearing a blues melody of debris
and gauze, a woman, and her dog. My half-
southern heart is a bruise shaped like daffodils.
My half-southern heart is full of names
shaped like smiles. The best cooking pot,
on the stove's front left eye, takes all
the ugly and all the song.

I have thickened grits with butter in winter,
after realizing I want to make love to a body
built for war—but has no need for war.

I have filled a plate in spring with grits
and mushrooms, or my mother's salmon patties
that taste like an eclipse—or catfish dropped
off by Frankie J cause he always has a hat
turned to the side. I have sat on cartons, stoops,
lawn chairs, sofa arms, and kitchen tables filled
with ceramic napkin holders and fake succulents.
I have spooned up years of grown-folk business
while keeping company with the moon.

Self-Portrait No. 7
(The Other Possible Self)

In one world I'm named Katherine
with a K and excel at hopscotch so
the players call me *slick feet*. I fall
in love with wheels of trucks and electric
trains. I stare at the way buoys can
shift water from indigo sound
to red warning. I like strawberries
and the gravelly texture of
oats on cream. Desire ripe artichokes
and numbers that pull juba from
teeth. I move to California where
the sun don't sleep. Dream
of being a conk hustler who pulls
nets onto the decks of ships,
or a cartographer who traces
the way the earth exhales. Still
craving the sluice of formulas, I
become an architect. I marry a guy,
our faces rest in dry frames. I have
adventures that bare no tears or
scars—just tines of forks scraping
plates.

Introvert Confessions

1

Sometimes when I enter a room, I pretend Zamunda is a real place. Everything in my view is petal-fused and brown-plated. No one is surprised by my eloquence or penchant for off-key song.

3

I pretend the phone is dying, so you can't hear me lie about wanting to go out.

8

A friend said humans are made out of dead stars. So technically we're not here all the time. Part of us is always searching, always elsewhere, using muscle memory to take us home.

9

Do birds have different dialects? Could a Brooklyn bird chirp to a Manchester bird? Or would there be confusion?

13

Fixating on grace, I try to learn the proper names for veins and which one leads to the left atrium. Egyptians wore wedding rings on the middle finger of the left hand, because that vein goes straight to the heart. My right hand is bigger than the left.

14

The blind intimidate me. There's too much investment
in touch. Their hands can see every rayless space
I've tried to hide. On sidewalks, do I offer to help
or by not helping do I hinder their passage? Anxiety
shivers the skin. In fear, I always cross the street.

17

I want every brown child to carry a red carpet
in their backpack or messenger bag. An unobtrusive
person will lay it down when they enter a room.
They'll strut like a spry beautiful hen, so they
never go phantom.

19

I worry about the darkest Huxtables. Did they
ever learn how to ask for what they want?
They were never too young for music, but
they couldn't dance the dark out.

21

There are odes to sun salutations but no poems
about Entenmann's on sale in winter. Everyone
has a favorite. How we teach the butter knife
to say *amen* over each slice.

25

I'll know our love is real when caution goes. You'll
be a howling heart I can touch and see. We be
brick and seashell with nails untrimmed. In the back-
ground, night will play our shadow on walls
like vowels in a R&B song.

What Answers Can I Give
to the Thing That I Am

• •

Once I tried to give away my shadow
but it refused to leave.
I could see it drowning but no one
could feel it asking for things—
to be taller
star-seared and loud
safe outside the wild hive of our skin.
Trying to find a thing called joy
or what we imagine joy feels like—
plate tectonics moving
a smile pulled from memory
of jumping in *exactly* the right moment
when playing double-dutch,
or a brown girl licking an ice cream cone,
her tongue a chameleon
and no boy or man makes a gesture
or says a word.
I think the shadow is the voice I hide.
I think I'm burying a voice in this poem.
The world is so loud
when I try to speak.
I see the silhouette of my sometimes
lover laying like he don't—
believe in God
anything absolute

or asking about my day
and the fact that my office suddenly
wants to talk about . . . diversity—
how does he see me?
A cocked table with lion clubbed
feet or a dark Gemini moon
that needs nothing
but comes when called.
I'm not his home, am I?
My shadow says you can't
lay down with a feral ellipsis
pretending to be a man.
Sometimes I think it's better to eat
chicken nuggets in bed half-
naked, rub turmeric
on my gums—turn to my shadow
for tenderness.

When I Tell Our Story
of Bees and Vinegar

I want to say—
    I don't know how
to be charming on an elevator
    or in any other place
where people avoid my eyes
    or watch my hands
like they're foreign soil—
    that walking outside is an erup-
tion of static
    everyone is talking or gasping
like fresh-pulled silver fish
    from a lake I've never seen—
that I constantly worry about
    the destiny of my organs
they work in tandem
    even the wild parts but
they can stop at any moment
    by choice or force—
that dear great-grandfather
    I have your crooked teeth
a birthmark shaped like
    a helicopter blade
your memories of how easy
    it is to lose land and refuge—

I want to say that we talk a lot
　　　but not about dreams
how they swell in buckets like
　　　language of flowers and all
the things we're too scared to say

Wishes for Black Folk in Woody Allen Movies

• •

Let them talk too fast about
cinema and the glory

of growing fire-escape basil,
or making the perfect south-

western omelet. Let them twirl
in the sun, a sultry quiet like

Jason's Lyric because the day
is lovely and their bills are paid.

The women board the A train,
fill it with their legs agape and wild.

Each body and smile takes
up three subway seats each.

They're not the best friend—
the you-go-girl hype man

the i-have-so-many-kids-
my-boobs-hang woman

or the i'm-from-the-streets girl
who never learned to read.

Let them be a hard pull of happiness.
Let them be uncomplicated and alive.

Red Salutations

I don't yet know how
        we got so heavy
with having red
and its children—
        vermillion fingernails
            firebrick ache
                rusted psalms
                        imperial gut pull
                              scarlet wishbone
                        chili wide-eye
                sienna trail
            burgundy songs
        and fire trees—
so much that we stay primed
for salt and seams
we hope never crack open

The wombs and fertility rates have noticed

We avoid dreams
        of maroon cardinals
            horses with blown pupils
                figures in top hats
                        floating ladders
                jackals
            splitting the pole
        and pretty sunsets

like they're all
ugly warnings

that not all galaxies
are allowed to breathe light
even in a house
of its own making

Endangered Species

I.

I went to the future
and color was gone

all the babies were pale
moon and bleach
fresh in the fist

no black man   no asian
woman or jew

just straight Tom's and Milky Way
sharp angles and blue-bone

II. Telegram

Meet the presses STOP year 2078 STOP the revolution is here STOP you can be white too STOP for just $19.99 STOP a pill for all that ails ya STOP re-grow skin and bone STOP re-write genetics STOP re-write history STOP connect your roots STOP straight to the *Mayflower* STOP documentation included STOP science is on our side STOP don't get left behind STOP you can be white too STOP STOP STOP

III.

I woke up in a field, full of
red poppies and ginger root

thin screams filled silver
paths to the brain

They had pulled out
the dark womb

chopped off my kinky hair
branches from my mama's tree

A voice asked, "Did you fall
from the sky sunburned?

Are there any more left like you?"

No Graveside Flowers

I want to dress you solely in memories—
wrap your body in movie lines
pull out those sounds of Leroy and *The Last Dragon*
    "When I say, Who's the master?!
    You say, Sho'nuff"
or your guilty pleasure of watching
Bewitched or *Charmed* cause who wouldn't want
to be a witch or warlock if asked.

I'm no witch but the child in me
wants to wash your skin
with Dove soap and keep you covered
in my pocket.

I know Mom wants you in a suit,
pressed and ready for God-
knows-what
but I brought your favorites—
a buckle with the silver dragon
and your Tootsie Pop shirt that asks
    "how many licks does it take . . ."

Respectful people would lay
roses or some other white carnation
over your heart
like a false blessing

pulling you pure and clean
but I promise to bring you a sparkly Michael
Jackson glove, rolls of Charleston Chews,
and Chick-O-Sticks.

Instead of the Baptist lament "eye on the sparrow"
with arms falling out, splayed mouths
of loved ones, I'll make it a party
and have a DJ spin all your classic hits.

I know I haven't dressed your feet yet,
boots, dress shoes, sneakers—I still can't
decide, little brother. Can we just sit here awhile?
Just sit here . . . until I figure it out?

Requiem for Sea and Chains

for the Middle Passage
after MAAFA Rebirth: *a photograph by Chester Higgins, Jr.*

who knew a body of water
   could be this large?

a mountain to the smallest
selves who made it
to the hulls alive
   their voices slipping
like a saffron bolt

at half-mast chains learned
not to scream
count heartbeats and swallow
   mouthfuls of dusk

the decks split open
as some leaped with the moon
   tossed their kinky
   manes in the sea

others fell to the dark
   spine and spirit broke
were tossed to the reefs like
open parasols while the sun
   looked on

praise the mists and bone-thief
holding our seeds on ocean floors

who knew water could swallow
       bodies so quietly?

B-Side Testimonials

I want to testify that the aunties were right. They were right
about having a spare $40 tucked in the rattiest bra you own—
to keep it there months in, no years in, just in case a bloom
goes sour and you gotta fly on the grey dog I mean grey-
hound for yourself or someone else. They were right about
how an onion bulb can save a half-priced Cornish hen. About
Sunday parsley and paprika. Ask your man if and when he
can taste either. I want to testify that sometimes you gotta
do battle with your scalp, the reflection in the mirror, then
your hair. Create a salve of lavender, peppermint, and red caster
oil. Don't rub it in like it's a sin or stain you gotta colonize.
Remember you're doing root work. Don't be afraid of the halo
your head can make. Let it be a sonnet dark or bright as Van Gogh's
Starry Night and yes you know Van Gogh. I want to testify
that I want more poems about pH balances and my cobalt X-
rays of fibroids that look like honey-glazed cakes. How a
body learns to accept the mass incarceration I mean intrusion.
I wish they were retractable gills or a coral storm gift for some
fantastical purpose. I want to testify that there ain't no glory
in being quiet and dignified. I want to testify that aging is
a motherfucker. I want to testify that I'm done with tasting
elegies in my mouth. Instead, I think of the 79 moons of Saturn,
give them proper names like Cletus, Chantal, and Ponyboy.
I want to testify that my fortune has not been told—despite
the world courting my curves to an end. I see the future

unfolding like an old school card catalog. Each card filled with dates, a shuffling of titles and days with lines pointing to all corners of the world, diagrams of humming blood relations. Each card smelling like a recipe or version of home.

In My Heaven

after Robin Coste Lewis

Everything begins with
hunger. Some crave Bartlett
pears, trees that breathe,
playing violin on gold roads.

Others only answer to their
animal names, knowing
which heart chamber calls

to the wolf, the sheep,
the jackal. In my heaven
currency are words—
people sing or recite

verb to noun to buy
burgers and cake, furniture
like wide-screen TVs

showing favorite programs
on loop with no commercials—
Soul Train, *I Dream of Jeannie*,
and *Happy Days*.

Each corner of heaven
is guarded by statues
of poets. They hold pens

as spears. When you rub
their stoned feet, you hear
dialects dipped in Marian
Anderson arias.

In my heaven Ms. Rose
plays the numbers
and hits every week.

Our shadows talk to other
shadows, have smoke-shaped
tea or whiskey at noon.

They visit bonfires to show their best forms
in the light. When you turn
18, 35, or 68 in my heaven,

you lay on a bed of tobacco
and ivy leaves. Stems shelter
as you're reborn, watching
stars fade into each other.

SIN IS A GOOD HYMN

My Calm App Lets Me
Sleep with Idris Elba

I.

This is my best waste of time—hearing a voice
tell a tale about a jungle when I'm
at the end of the world.
I remember my right to breathe,
that the body knows how to unfurl—
imagine its tongue could carve
a castle out of a mountain.
Dear Manufactured Calm,
we get used to being whelmed over.
I got a face that's never at rest
but Idris's voice makes me want things—
a brother to grow old with lines of smiles
a necklace of dry watermelon seeds
or a welcome-heated hand that coils a thigh goose
bump birthing.

II.

Some days it's easier to remember that
even the devil needs someone to love,
to find soft moons in the edges
crooning words like a downwind river—
so we forget his hard hands at work.
When I watched the TV show *Bewitched* I thought

Darrin must've had great dick—
the James Earl Jones of dick
the kind of dick where you're almost naked
while wearing one sock and a headwrap.
To make a woman hide herself—
hide her daughter like she's a knotted
ball of hair, of sorrys, and a nose full of questions.
How can a man be unhappy when
his woman is magic? I want to ask my
mother this. Or my dead grandmother
in a dream cause I've heard her story
second- and thirdhand.

III.

Idris is now talking about owls and ancient
rock art like it's something sacred
we ripened together.
I believe him
and almost forget my day
of basement apartment laundry—hauling
my back, black roots
clothes, and a key chain of blue
pepper spray. The maintenance man—
I mean devil I mean nice man,
asks for my hand and body every time I see him.
One day I think he'll say *no* to my
no thank you. He'll want to break something—
he'll want to sing to something that's broken;
pry it without a key.

Challenged echoes learn how to rescue
themselves—so I keep my spray
loose, swallow my spit
think of calm and Idris—
crooked paths to my cotton nightdress.

Recipe for Keeping a Man

* *

eastern potatoes

is the first wish. the first language offered
from the ground. prone to brine and settle
the stomach, liver, and lungs like a ceiba
tree. knowledge rests here. this is what
God gave.

aluminum pans

never fear a reaper or audience. it's all
about heft. can it stay stolid. take mass into
all four corners of its heart and hold a floor
steady. can its body grip, like a pallbearer's
palm, a man's center without shaking at the
root.

paprika

curls like a scarlet vine on the tongue and
you quickly forget freshwater fish and sugar
cane pulled from fists. see this new master
coming to greet them. linger. carry its red
flag on teeth until it has conquered the
kitchen.

relish

is the side of right. all the grandmas are gone
but they murmur in throats and ladles
of cracked wooden spoons. *don't fear the
tart bits, honey.* it's the grandmothers
calling you home. showing you the right
way to stir a man pickled.

mayonnaise

can plug a hole and heal a hearth. slick a
thorn from any rib. there are many songs in
the minor key. each has a gift for sniffing
out weakness. binds the secrets you want to
keep.

mustard

bitters the barbeque. breaks bread with
aunts and ants like bees around
blossoms. a waterfall of smoke sneaks into
hair. light descends through the knees.

eggs

was the second wish. potato salad the
third. an unsuspecting target dances with
plastic fork in hand. joy falls from his
skin. he wants to live in this shimmy. the
heat is like being in the womb again.

I Want to See Black
Love on Television

Be camera. Be kaleidoscope. Quicksilver in the front room
where everything is worn but you can smell tea tree oil or
cinnamon from something bought not baked. I like the word
languish, Crystal Waters, and bass. I decide to add a man or
woman to my diet. We argue about trash day and whose turn
it is. Something sparkles loose-limbed. See the first smile then
the third. Be the lens of my gaze at the stove during winter.
I like buying things on sale; wear matching pajamas that
are good for dancing. Or maybe I can't dance at all. I have
no rhythm, I just sway back and forth like an acolyte to the
morning. All of my bills are paid. I have braids the right length
to pull yourself in. Life lines in my hand are strong; I know
how to reach for stars I can keep. Enjoy a green smoothie from
the vendor on Smith. All of my brothers are alive and free.
Fear touches the air around their clothes but they don't let it
in. The hard pull of people is what feels like home. At night I
like Ritz crackers dipped in tea cause it's what my father ate.
I think about getting a turtle named Jon Jon. I'm a cougar for
men who play an instrument. With sex there's heat in every
thunder, an avalanche rising. I don't have a sassy white friend
who talks too much about the wrong things. There's a run in my
stockings but I don't care. I'm trying to fit all parts of myself—
grandfather's wet sea pearls, my mother's windowsill aloe,
knowledge that dark-colored feathers are strong and fray less.

What Can Grow in the Dark

One day I will enter your arms
        and be swallowed
into untamed yeast
        and Sunday barley

we'll be slick as sweat
        from frosted soda cans

we'll forget the good-
        byes we say in doorways
and subway platforms

the myths about hair
        and bathroom drains

killing centipedes because
        one thing should not have
that many legs

or who can tell lies
        more deeply about
how much care is required
        to maintain us

but today I smell you
        in a crowded room like

there's no space
      between our houses

and our tiny kingdom
      in a wet Jersey night
asks for nothing

Self-Portrait No. 9
(What the Mirror Sees)

• •

In this world my mother names
me Cynthia, after the goddess
of the moon. She creates a lullaby
called *step to the Cindy Cindy Cindy*

and reads me books about magical
creatures. I fall in love with words
and I'm tethered to the why of *every-*
thing—the way a flag waves air

and how the syllables of *blueberries*
and *plethora* undress, ripen around
the tongue. I am so hungry for
what I don't know, my wisdom

teeth grow back every year.
I search cemeteries because some
engravings are carved deeper than
others. The sky soaks up my blues.

I enjoy being called ruthless, replying
under my breath *"those yeasty bitches."* I
curve my hand like the letter "C," trace
vena cava, fuck—like a pussy freed.

Praise for Luke Cage's Skin and Starshine

• •

You know what it's like to be night
all the time, don't you? Others have
        to wait for that artificial glow
via backlight or tanning booth. But you
    are an element that can't be spliced,
            quantified. I like you bulletproof
    and free, you make wanting to live
a life legal, where eyes can stay wide and
    hungry, not sad.

        Everywhere you go black boys
    follow, try to scoop the cells
            and selves left behind. Some have
tiny magnifying glasses and mini plastic
            cups. And when something is found,
    they watch it like seeds ready to sprout
            wings or leaves of comic book power.
    Others take their loot, rub it along their
hairline and edges like it's part pomade,
            part starshine.

And I resist the urge to join the queue.
        Cause those light-skinned boys keep
their love too high for my skin's reach.
        Your Cage would have me moon rapt,

wondering how a rooster moans,
and if my own father ever thought I
            was beautiful. We'd walk through Harlem—
you in a fitted suit, and me wearing
    anything-I-damn-well-please, until
            rain or movie magic turns us
    into one body, the right shade of
            Bernie Mac black.

Something Like Gratitude
to the Girl on the 5 Train

• •

       Your earbuds whispered
   that's the way love goes
     and Janet smooth-
  crooned on my left side, base-lining
capillaries stirring something
   starved, like a muffled drum.
I remember the brown video abs
   every girl wanted to see in mirrors.
       How some twisted
     their short dark torsos back, forth
  in hope and benediction.
Some claimed she had a rib removed
  to cinch that Jackson waist.
       The track switches to "Rhythm Nation."
I taste strawberry-kiwi Mystic drinks
   plantain chips—my go-to after-school
      cuisine. My short ponytail is slicked
  with pink lotion. My parents talk
to each other in cold syllables. My sister
   is away at college and the house is heavy.
   I stomp out confusion with
      combat boots, silver chains, braided
  lanyards attached to my bag
     like an opening anthem.
Back then Janet's eyes were hard,

hid what it meant to be tender.
Who knows what demons and land
    truths she had conquered? The train
        stops and you, Janet, and 1994 depart—
    but my shadow flickers, follows
with a choreographed dance number.
    It feeds me muscle memory, the name
        of a skinny boy who kissed
    like wet elephant grass,
        and lines for this poem.

Dear Superman

Tell yourself what you will
that you wait patiently
to tip your Clark hat and jaw
to every Sara, Lois, or bright-
haired Jane. Women with coiffed
hair, pink lips, and cosmetics
lightly placed. Delicate shades
that blush oh so nicely on paper,
TV, and high-resolution film.
But I see how the animal
of your body passes by
the dark girls. Girls with names
like Esther, Jaleesa, or Cantina
Rose. Girls who wear glasses
and dresses with the slip showing.
Women of strong flavors—
hot peppers between their legs
and a storm inside. Those girls
secretly stir you from liver to toenail.
And they too crave strong arms—a cape
to cradle inside, and have dreams
of sleeping between stars.

List Poem for Things I Try to Love . . .

— okra with its slime
— cooked eggs that are neither completely solid
    or liquid aka poached
— candy corn
— basically all foods in different shades of yellow
— poems about cats named King, Felix,
    or Abraham
— Scrabble when I pull the letter "Q"
— Scrabble when I hide the letter "Q" in my sock
— songs ended abruptly by talking DJs
— the uniboob in supportive bras that don't
    support attractiveness
— my oily skin that sometimes feels like a slip-n-slide
— my mother when she calls her unmarried daughter
    on a Friday night
— absent fathers who resemble stars with
    working cell phones
— my uterus when it feels like a horde of gladiators
    in a closed ring
— skin tags shaped like tiny almonds
— the realization that even the softest men have edges
— my size 11 feet when they feel like mini steamboats
— people who video-call as a surprise
— when my words forge a bonfire
— poetry when pain is its default setting
— when strangers assume I have multiple children

— when non-strangers ask when I'm having multiple
        children
— my body rolls pre-Spanx
— my body rolls when trying to remove sweaty Spanx
— my lover when he mansplains yeast infections
        because he knows how to google
— Uno when a bitch to my left puts down draw 4
— myself when I'm tired
— myself every day

After That Night:
Medusa Calls Out Poseidon

for Patricia Smith

● ●

I don't ask for much just
enough room to fall back
into your grace—that hot
spot reserved for
communion wafers
or your favorite ginger chews,
the kind that anchor behind
the right molar and you puff
your tongue to taste for hours.
Yes, you know how to leave—
how to turn away from collarbone,
rib cage, and these snake-eyes,
but the you in my mind is full of
heart-stops and half-speak. Like
that night at Coney Island,
popcorn hands and bits of caramel
apple stuck to our white dove cloaks,
like candied worms bright as rogue
flowers, and there was no fault
to be found. Our palms were read
and the lifelines split at the same place—a
stone in a river, bending currents
just for our sake. I know you
wake at dawn to work and rule,

just like I know the right way to
unfold your skin like
an indigo tarp or cuttlefish. See
me in your chariot mirror and
be not afraid. Can't you feel me
there? In that bone hull over the
god's heart?

Dear Sunflowers Who Congregate Without a Permit

for Ada Limon

Twenty to thirty is too large a number to gather
without air-conditioning. Fifteen of you
dazzle, others bow their heads, too burdened,
too rough, with no yellow-gold to be found.
Their children collapse to the ground as if
they could never get warm enough and
a woodland social worker is removing them
from their care. I want to curl in a leaf like
an Anne Geddes photograph. But those babies
must be propped or photoshopped because
nothing alive can be that lovely, not even us.
I'm supposed to be writing about nature but—
a little boy sings *upside down, boy, you turn me*, the
bees are a Greek tragedy waiting to happen and
this bird reminds me of a Jamaican cabdriver
yelling out *Flatbush Flatbush Utica next stop.*
I'm sorry for not singing enough, and making
salmon patties in your favorite pan when I know
you hate fish. Some apologies sound like
the word *home.* Can't you hear my hunger,
bright as this gang of flowers?

Elegy to a Portrait of Us Where You're Smiling and I'm Looking Away

• •

The reed in your throat is mine, he says.
The coyote hour of red clay and jawbone is mine, he says.
That brown ankle in the sea, covered in silver chains and blue
    charms, *I bought that*, he says.
Your heart, liver, and lungs all in one volume belongs to me,
    he says.

I took *I will enter you* as a challenge.
I took the you in my mind and added milk.
I took the you in my mind and added gasoline
to make a voodoo doll that dances when lit.
But sometimes I'm afraid of anything that is too big—
sex that resembles a spell,
love that arrives caged.

So I eat mangoes in December,
suck their sweet each rising
like a new type of church or lighthouse.
I shake off your scent and markings
like a small animal.

Message Pulled from a Bottle at Sea

—*after* The Little Mermaid

Dear Ms. Ursula,
you remind me of Aunt Odessa.
She used to laugh loud and outside
all the seagulls would scatter.
She liked to wear dresses that made
noise when she walked,
like little bells you see at parades.

But she hated kids who whined, people
who were skinny as sticks, and she
never celebrated Halloween.

Mama says she needs to learn to love
herself and that's why she's mean. Do you
love yourself, Ms. Ursula? Is that
why you're mad? Did the sea
leave you behind?

I think you and Odessa get a bad rap
and you're real pretty, like those
opera singers on TV. Your voice
is nice too. Those jazz records we play
on Saturdays gots nothin on you.

Uncle Toby says, *meat on the bone
is where it's at*, but Mama—she
always tells him to *hush*.

Dear Spring,

I've decided to take Love for a walk—
far from my allegiance to lighting and howls
away from TV trials about humanity,
where love barely survives.
The dog upstairs is yapping about nothing
and curry from my neighbors' pot drifts
onto my nightstand.
What can seeds teach us about holding?
I'm allergic to your peonies your
hell fever I mean hay fever,
pollen dense enough for me to ask,
"are all these bees fucking except me?"
but then I remember
that's not how pollination works.
So I turn my Love to seeing
for I am always thirsty
for a kiss in high heels
and a finger trailing in the dark.
I once told an ex that Häagen-Dazs
was like orgasms—there is never
enough. But I should've said love
and night and spring and moonshine
where maidens aren't the rescued—
but the takers of prey.

Last Night Inside My Blood

I was scent-starved
for oranges in winter.
Wanting pips and half-
hearts to burst.
Send my nose
to that August
in Ireland,
where I was free
from rules of kin
and what good girls
should do.

There was a boy
with steady fingers
and arms well-veined,
a hollow-body guitar
like a black sword
on his back.
He called me C
I called him B,
and that's how he got me—
consonants, not vowels.
In a jazz fest full
of downbeats,
with pints of Bulmers,
he knew how

to peel my rind
like a Marabel potato.
All in one go.

He didn't stop
to breathe or make
pit-tale promises
like crumpled orchids.
He peeled so
our birth cut
like a trade wind,
our sternums
barely covered
and wild.

We Make Sin a Good Hymn

• •

After a game of Spades
it's as if my wild hairs
are Braille or wet
dandelion grass unbristled

It's a wonder how you move
like there's house
whiskey or wine in your veins

I get so drunk off the dark
galaxies under our skin
it rushes like major keys
or brass cello horns

We take turns reading finger
twists and temple fades
there's an entire ecosystem
beneath the nails

I peel a tangerine
its spray another kiss
and you brown pelican
collect the rinds

They splay the bed
like new languages or
flowers still in their fields

Forget coyote hour
the meetings we have tomorrow
pots brimmed over
every clock
this house
is light-headed

IF WE SHOULD,
WHO WILL FLY AFTER US

a white co-worker asks if my family sits down to have frank discussions about race

• •

I say we're long-time investors in the business of care-taking, knowing where the shovel is and how many minutes it takes. *asiatic lilies.* Pavement markers/chalk lines spring into fashion every other week. Do disasters have other names? *button poms.* Newsmen love to strip a phrase to looting. To kill it quiet, you have to act like it's easy as blinking or memorizing multiplications. 12 x 12 = 144 lashes. *green hydrangeas.* A professor asks me to write about the murmurations of starlings. But I don't give a fuck about starlings or cranes or crickets. My worldview is open enough to see scarecrows on fire, a roach on its back, rat-birds fighting over bone and wrapper. *larkspur. snapdragons.* You've received work bonuses how many times? *gerbera daisies.* In meetings my tone always contains drama or debris pressed down. I'm Black all the time. I'm going off-site tomorrow. I'll be sure to put my braids in a bun. *swan wing tulips.* Once at a college crossroads, a friend said the war between the states was unnecessary. Plantation owners were just waiting for financial stability. *chrysanthemums.* Some squad cars have mastered the slow pass, it's like a rolling stop but amplified with *bed bait bed bait and ooo-wee look at all that dark candy* if your breasts are brown. if your breasts are large and brown. *palm fronds.* Outtakes turn intakes if your black back is wide, sneakers wild, if you talk too tough, too smart, too loud. Fear is *queen anne's lace. baby's breath. oriental lilies. pale carnations.*

Things I Will Tell My Children

• •

You will always remind them
of weighted tumbleweeds,
hen-egg brown.

There's a ragtime beneath your skin.
It stirs earth's curvature
and a choir of frogs
when you enter or leave a room.

Don't leave a swallow of juice
or milk in the fridge.

Always remember that a body
grieved is a whole new body.

Give your shadow a name
big as a star, so you can see
yourself out loud.

Pick wild irises. The best gifts
roll under a rib cage, leave
open mouths splendid.

I like your smile unpenned.
Keep your birdsong close.

Imagine an hourglass full
of architects and dreamers,
the first taste of fresh-
scooped ice cream.

You will learn to master camouflage
among ordinary things—
men who spill words
not thoughts, trigger fingers
ready to brand loose.

I love your smile unpenned.

One Vow After the Other

Let me had been
the star watching that night
in 1978,
the rain battering the building
like a child yelling *More! More! Again!*
or the moth in the corner of the
room like the best shadow,
as my parents discussed the idea
of me, child number two.
Maybe they held hands
tight as a mast
trying to make the grip permanent.
Was their talk of money?
Pluses and minuses in a column—
her at home stretching change,
him in his black-and-blue truck
driver gear unloading petals,
or was it like Edison's first light
when the air seared
the collarbone flexed
and the lips curved?
Let me had been perched
on the wall
before their heart was
fully formed for me.

I would've said *take heed*—
you're making another vow with love,
she'll be born with crooked legs,
wait—they'll be days she'll feel like a
weed, not a dandelion.

A Taste of Blue

• •

I tell my father about the way
I collect small things
in the sacs of my heart—

thick juniper berries
apple cores that retain their shape
and the click of shells
that sound like an oven baking.

He presses the mole on my shoulder
that matches his shoulder,
proof that I was not found
at the bottom of the sea.

I also got his feet, far from
Cinderella's dainty glass slippers—
and fingers, too wide for most

Cracker Jack wedding rings.
I read how some mammals never
forget their young—

their speckled spots, odd goat
cries, or birthmarks on curved
ivory tusks. There must be some

thread of magic there
cooling honey to stone—
where like recognizes like or
how a rib seeks its twin.

The Way the World Holds You

Have you seen the city trees
as beckoned palms too often empty?
Something green pulls you to place
hands on bark, rub feet against it like
Bengal tigers or emery boards.
Some people just see the waiting coil
of subway tracks, something scurrying
out the corner of one's eye, but home is
a collection of rowan branches.

      I am a braided brown girl walking.
      Some men say, *hey, sweetie, give us*
      a smile, ask where I'm headed—
      hold the front of their jeans like
      their dicks weigh seven pounds. Others
      say I have a house party on my hips.
      I hear the hollow points and my breath
      isn't graceful. I imagine a tall helix armor
      filled with amaranth and apple skins—
      wear it like a suit when needed.

Witness the constellation of windows,
broom-filled cupboards, showers of
merengue ballads on Friday nights
and mumbling moans of tilted mouths.
Some are fighting, others are pixels
of colors as God clears her throat.

I wonder if we're really just things
science has yet to define—stars with
people names, winter moth wings
in disguise, or undissolvable elements
that just got too big.

There Are No Unsacred Spaces

I'm trying to tell you that—the world is beautiful.
All the hellos we say in a week, or month, the way
the grooves of the grin know what to do. Think
about the first time man went from four legs, hairy
knuckles folded over, to two. The moment the spine
realized it could brace against its cage. That the bones
wouldn't splinter or spark; the sound that escaped.
From that height, where did the eyes look first? I bet
He wondered about who feeds the sun. Who can
stand next to him. I'm trying to tell you—something
about the universe. If you connect each lake and
ocean with a pencil, they mirror constellations.
The barking stars are like dimes. They know about
the tenderness of orcas, as if their size were made
to contain opposites, like we contain opposites.
They know that the surf never takes everything, a body
always documents where its been down to the horse-
shoe crab. I'm trying to tell you that—it's okay to curse
God a little. That your mother keeps giving you
plants that you overwater or underwhelm. To crest
burden over joy, piss over water, 'cause hurt can get
so loud sometimes. I'm trying to tell you that—history
doesn't begin with language, with words on top of
words. It begins with skin, and wonder, and touch—
like that dating app with welders and endangered

blacksmiths. They enter every unlit space with their craggy nicked hands; then carve the letter A from the shape of an ox.

Self-Portrait No. 13 (What's Passed Down in the Making)

● ●

Sometimes I smile just like
my mother,
as if the skin and gums
remember the day I was born,
between thick thighs and
southern jasmine.
With a second toe
larger than the first,
I arrived as a red-throated
anthill, just as busy.
And maybe the moon was
in my half-blind eyes
but I felt what was handed down—
stories in the water
darkling skin luminous
grandmother's brass comb, its
teeth well used,
a bowl of awe and root
veins of an ancient path
stumbles into prayers to put me
on the side of right,
and the galloping heart
of a jukebox.

But what did my mother dream?
When she knew how much hunger
the dark could contain.
How close we are to
mindsets behind—
plantation-born juleps
foxes in the henhouse
kissing caskets,
knowledge that we use our bones
to hold up more
than just our bodies.

She saw a girl—using
stones and light
hands learning the art of
pepper oil
hair braiding like a rope
to free oneself
the tones of hand games
to sense when a voice is
off—and bare feet striding
a ground bursting with
fire tulip lips

When You Kiss a Smoker

• •

My gums crave cinder and ash like whole milk
and pear trees. The scent spins like a pack of
bees high off steam in a pattern my brain can't
or won't forget, so I seek it out—

>   like midnight rides when
>   the air is quiet, a dark house party in a friend's
>   basement, or hot prayers under a blanket
>   where the breath goes clumsy.
>   Men

with parched lips and Newports, musicians
with long fingers on break by a propped side door,
one cigarette in hand posing like a question, the other
tucked behind an ear, a dark rose unbloomed. I think, *this*

>   *is what love is*, a scent with promise and no
>   real name, but I smelled it in my father's hug,
>   tight as moon pit when I didn't know fear.

I Could Be a Boxer

I have a history
of growing back wisdom
teeth, parting my gums

like persimmon fruit
and making it look easy.
Like bright dead things

look easy or carving
S.O.S. in fresh cement,
the branch moving

like arms or legs.
But I know my body—
it's a stove that learned

early how to bake
a life or take one.
Like mending a crow's

wing when I was eight,
its feathers thick
enough to fill an urn.

And birthing that tooth?
was like punching out
a bruised rib but

I took it like God
was in my throat
telling me not to cede.

#45 Presidential Vibrations

at work they talk of taxonomies
        how words create bubbles
    of conversation   matter
we breathe   out newsfeeds each rising
    swallow its burnt thistle
until everyone is on the same page
        homogeneous white wonder
    bread   on top of unlined paper
no safe   words   just trauma museums
    about who and what   matters
when it comes to funding   female bodies curled
    like a fig   man-made grassy knolls with
    little grass   but I sometimes think *no*   these rooms
    are too small   the doors kaleidoscope and move
there isn't enough light   for us   this conversation
    it's always starless here   I say where
are all the gone things   not pretty enough for bows

Notes Toward a Poem
on Self-Care . . .

• •

start with decisions—take a break from mirrors . . .
decide to stay in bed today and tomorrow . . . count
time only through midnights . . . isn't there some voodoo
about being the middle child of a middle child? . . . you
should google that . . . start humming . . . to broken bones
of electrical appliances . . . that old CD player? yep you can
fix it . . . take on do-it-yourself projects—face cream, shelves,
the perfect guacamole, and a *Home Alone* arsenal just in case
a Joe Pesci–like villain tries to arrive . . . pretend the varnish
brush is a stag horn . . . who needs an app for calm?? . . . be
greedy about breathing . . . be greedy about breathing . . . avoid
phone conversations and relate only through yes and no texts
or emails . . . *hey baby, can you be my Melanin Maid Marion?*
yes! . . . *does   have a job?* oh no girl . . . *is your brother/
father/husband accounted for?* . . . (silence) . . . yes . . . if voice
is required, realize that he/she/they can't be your Sun . . . trust
what you can hold in the hand . . . when we talk the body
vibrates . . . aim for a dinosaur roar when people least expect it
. . . enjoy words like *Kilimanjaro* and *origami* . . . write odes to
the Durag . . . sonnets to the *Soul Train* line where you dance
in military choreographed precision . . . so fresh and so clean
Outkast, *take a look it's in a book, Reading Rainbow* . . . Jolly
Ranchers, your mother's kitchen table . . . at any altitude
remember that ink can hold the right kind of memory . . .

Seeking Language for Peaches or Joy

• •

Should you find me
falling into the earth,
don't be alarmed—
it's just my spine
trying to climb
back into peach vines
or the nearest brown womb.

Some know the first taste
of homegrown peaches, Nina
Simone's Peaches,
and how freedom
is just a feeling but
I felt that once—
that day at Coney Island

where my father's truck driver
pockets held bruised
peaches, brown-spotted
like the inside cover
of a matchbook.

We sat after Skee-Ball
with my chin dripped sweet,

his hands holding
a small orange giraffe.
I even sucked on the pit—

bitter and shaped like a bird's
heart. But it was mine,
like my father was mine,
and that day was ours.

Self-Portrait No. 11
(Climatology in Flux)

• •

Your current age feels like a polar
jet stream, the joy of bills paid, the pop
and fizzle of name-brand aged wines.

You now have a clear start to shock
and denial of dropped arches, joints
in need of patching after dancing

in red 3-inch heels. You are done
with thunderstorms that rolled through
your twenties, you've swallowed rain

shadows with eucalyptus leaves.
A woman without cares has plenty
of time for bridesmaid dresses

and office baby showers. *Did you sign
Sarah's card? Have you thought about
freezing your eggs?* The low will be a 30%

chance of tears after a heat wave with
loose-loving men, hard-boiled goods
too much alive. Beware of depression

disguised as barometric pressure.
Or El Niño, those friendly people
who call you momma or mami
because you're brown and round. It leads

to flip-flops, binge-eating frosted marble
cake, and old-school musicals. *Dear
Conrad Birdie, you can still get it.*

All your stories sit in trees and in credit
scores. The high will be a southern
oscillation—knowledge that you can be
wind too wild for taming if you choose.

Things I Can't Say in This Book

● ●

1. Gallop, conquistador, racist, yearning, heartfelt, rose, Gertrude Stein, *Shaft*, jive turkey, Richard Roundtree, insouciant, and alabaster
2. Flies, gnats, and bees want *my* blood especially
3. There should be a starter kit for women featuring coconut oil, duct tape, judo lessons, and a switch blade that doubles as corkscrew, bottle opener, and flat-head screwdriver
4. In dreams I taste hurricanes. I am never full
5. I fear my brother, your brother, and his brother are vessels for gunpowder
6. I'm agnostic but small green Bibles the size of palms make me jealous; I think it's the promises they try to keep
7. I don't give a fuck about carbs
8. Something red is buried in my hello, it's probably anger
9. Will I lose Black points if I'm not angry enough?
10. You know, you're really attractive when you're asleep and not talking
11. The adult palate misses fried baloney that dimples in the middle
12. Some questions hurt more than answers, just ask Dr. King, Jesus, and Freddie Gray
13. No, Cynthia isn't an ethnic name and I *do* sound cultured on the phone
14. There are a hundred words for joy; how many do you use?
15. Dear Crayola, your 64-crayon pack is lacking multicultural options, i.e., cinnamon, cocoa, sepia, tan, and mahogany

16. Dear *Jetsons*, *Flintstones*, and *DuckTales*, if you have negro handmaidens or nannies hidden in your basement, just out of camera view, please release them at once, or have we all been exterminated?

All of My Rejected and Broken Poems Come Together and Form a Gang

One leads the stride and others trail behind
two by three
then three by four
they like to roll into places wide-hipped
with letters spread
taking up every inch of spit, breath, and train seat
they sometimes use the moon as a map
roam bookstores
are compelled to give words to strangers
crawl into libraries
ear hustle unsuspecting offices
cause they know how to code-switch
snip metaphors and similes in one breath
be as Black as language demands in another
they each have purpose
the poem about camels?
knows to cover the flank of every literary submission
another poem called "The Unkindness of Red"
knows how to cut the product
slice potential lines to be used for others
the Aunt Jemima poem is part den mother part historian
she keeps records of the OGs
the first in the crew who thought they'd be alone forever

but now have family
the haikus are the strangest
written during 30/30 in April
they have short attention spans
dream in colors that don't exist
born unnamed they know that named things are rarely slain
they are a blush of parts
kept medicated and sandwiched between others
the newest poems think they have muscle
and won't be here long
they peel open beehives
serve as runners with their vowels shimmying
like a centipede ready to level up and out
but the real power lies in the tall lean poems
those trying to build a nest or trampoline
they hold memories tight enough that every body
they touch is haunted
they know a spoonful of ink
makes the medicine go down

Self-Portrait No. 15
(Interrogation Under the Moon)

* *

State Your First Name

It depends on which version of me you need to see.
which side is at the ready, corporate me, 9-to-5 me,
sister me, hustler me, daughter me, lover me, wet me,
New York me, lustful me, annoyed me, Gemini me.

Daughter/Son of

Leo the lion, the middle child of a middle child.
in *Book of Beasts*, when a lioness gives birth to
her cubs, she rings them forth dead and lays them
lifeless for three turns of a moon. on the third day,
the father arrives from doing god-knows-what,
breathes in their faces and they come alive. some
cubs are born with crooked legs, others with teeth.

Who Loves

Almond trees. blankets in the color blue. earrings
that dangle in odd shapes. the wildness inside all
of us. good whiskey and so-so bourbon in tea.
what the collarbone knows when I'm with you.
the phrase "listen here home slice."

Who Hates

Pits of plums and avocados. rage without reason.
the way a black hurt isn't loud. the way a black love

isn't loud. cheesecake. email purgatory. dreams
about crooked teeth. poems where commas perch
like an afterthought. the smell of pressed flowers
that remind me of funeral Bibles.

Who Needs

Dollar pizza slices where you can taste the basil.
Home-Goods. poems that become spells or a
recipe. permission to take naps. Walgreens with
a short line and a nice cashier. dreams about
grandmothers. the love letters between the page
and me.

Who Feels

When the moon is full like a song at the tip of
my tongue. the scabbed knee I received at age
6. like I don't got time to rage, I have work in
the morning. sugarcane and fire. anxiety like a
skipped record on a turntable.

Who Fears

The light I can't hold inside. how our story will
end. hollow seeds. cracked eggs with multiple
yolks. black limbs uncoordinated like a bird
opening its chest. hairless cats.

Who Would Like to See

Soul sanctuaries in every city. they'll be speakeasies
where Black folk will flee office microaggressions,
regular aggressions, the Karens, the newsreels,
and statistics that serve only the reporters not the

reported. the sanctuaries would be free, playing unheard riffs from Thelonious Monk, the B sides of Motown records, and live studio sessions of Prince. it would offer free massages, Beyoncé yoga, and workshops on wealth and folding fitted sheets.

Acknowledgments

Dear Reader, wherever you are, think about a time when you thought *I'm glad to be alive*. This moment can be banal or fantastical, at the present time or in memory. For me it's family and my mother making salmon patties and grits or taking me to the Macon Library to get books as a child, my brother and I laughing about movies and impersonating Vanity from *The Last Dragon*, and it's my sister giving me sage advice and not getting mad when I ignore it.

It's moments and places where ideas are born: Cave Canem is a bouquet of daffodils and hard poems; the long walk from Chapman Studio at MacDowell while carrying a picnic basket and being afraid of rustling deer; the writer's suite at Saltonstall Foundation where I wished the trees could speak of history; the balcony at the Château de la Napoule with a view of the sea and its dining room where we gathered to watch Beyonce's *Homecoming*; and it's the studio at Monson Arts where I tacked poems on the wall while recovering from a snow squall in March.

It's also the people that come with the poems, the writing community and group chats. To those who give feedback on poems after midnight—JP Howard and Emily Blair; to those who gave feedback on this manuscript—Lolita Stewart White and Steven Leyva; to the 92nd Street Y crew led by Nathalie Handal who encouraged me to write about love; and to the literary magazines and organizations who contribute to the community pot of poetry, including the Barbara Deming Memorial Fund, Elizabeth Sloan Tyler Memorial Award via

Woven Tale Press, Frontier Poetry, and Furious Flower—
I thank you.

Lastly, it's also the intangible and the little things that guide me—the whisper of ancestors that say *no, don't go that way* or *yes, grab that moment*; the paths forged by literary ancestors; my contemporaries who become unofficial mentors by existing; and the people who check on their "strong friends"—you all make me think *I'm so glad to be alive.*

Credits

AGNI—"There Are No Unsacred Spaces"

Argos (Calendar)—"Dear Sunflowers Who Congregate Without a Permit"

The Baffler—"One Vow After the Other"

Bear Review—"Self-Portrait No. 11 (Climatology in Flux)"

Bone Bouquet—"No Graveside Flowers" and "Self-Portrait No. 1 (On Becoming Light)"

Box of Jars—"I Try to Imagine Them Smitten"

Callaloo—"a white co-worker asks if my family sits down to have frank discussions about race"

Catapult—"Is This Your Sky or Mine?"

Clockhouse—"MTA Transit Exam Attempt #4" and "Seeking Language for Peaches or Joy"

Columbia Journal—"After That Night: Medusa Calls Out Poseidon," "Pretending Is Like Breathing," and "3 am and the Moon is Curled like a 'C'"

Cortland Review—"Dear Superman"

Cosmonauts Avenue—"Introvert Confessions" and "Praise for Luke Cage's Skin and Starshine"

Emotive Fruition—"We Make Sin a Good Hymn" and "What Can Grow in the Dark"

Foundry—"Notes Toward a Poem on Self-Care . . ." and "#45 Presidential Vibrations"

Frontier Poetry—"Self-Portrait No. 5 (Phoenix and Lullabies)"

Great Weather for Media Anthology—"Elegy to a Portrait of Us Where You're Smiling and I'm Looking Away"

Hyperallergic—"I Could Be a Boxer"

IthacaLit—"Ode to *JET* Magazine (When You Be a Rainbow with a Streak of Black)"

LA Presa—"Girls Like Me Are Made Of . . ."

LARB—"Self-Portrait No. 13 (What's Passed Down in the Making)"

New York Underwater (Broadside)—"Requiem for Sea and Chains"

Nine Mile—"In My Heaven," "Recipe for Keeping a Man," and "When You Kiss a Smoker"

No Dear—"I Want to See Black Love on Television"

Obsidian—"All of My Rejected and Broken Poems Come Together and Form a Gang," "I Wish the Trees Could Sway to Marvin and Aretha," and "Something Like Gratitude to the Girl on the 5 Train"

Pluck!—"Endangered Species"

Poem-a-Day—"A Taste of Blue" and "Things I Will Tell My Children"

Poets House—"I Learned to Be a Lady"

Public Pool—"Message Pulled from a Bottle at Sea," "Rx for Little Black Girls," and "Things I Can't Say in This Book"

The Shallow Ends—"Baby, What's Your Favorite Body Part?"

Sink Review—"When I Tell Our Story of Bees and Vinegar"

VIDA Review—"Dear Future Body (Keep Your Skin Thickk)" and "The Way the World Holds You"

Wildness—"Urban Tumbleweed"

Wordpeace—"Litany for My Fears and Questions"

Zócalo Public Square—"How You Livin?"

About the Author

Cynthia Manick is the editor of *The Future of Black: Afrofuturism, Black Comics, and Superhero Poetry* (Blair Publishing, 2021) and *Soul Sister Revue: A Poetry Compilation* (Jamii Publshing, 2019), and the author of *Blue Hallelujahs* (Black Lawrence Press, 2016). She has received fellowships from Cave Canem, Hedgebrook, MacDowell, and Château de la Napoule among others. Winner of the Lascaux Prize in Collected Poetry, Manick is founder of the reading series Soul Sister Revue, which she created in 2014. A storyteller and performer at literary festivals, universities, and museums, Manick's work has appeared in the Academy of American Poets Poem-a-Day Series, *Catapult*, *Los Angeles Review of Books*, *The Wall Street Journal*, and elsewhere. She currently resides in Brooklyn, New York.